THE TRUE COST OF TECHNOLOGY

HOW TO SHOP TO CHANGE THE WORLD

Mary Colson

CRABTREE
Publishing Company
www.crabtreebooks.com

Crabtree Publishing Company

www.crabtreebooks.com
1-800-387-7650

PMB 59051,
350 Fifth Ave., 59th Floor
New York, NY 10118

616 Welland Ave.
St. Catharines, ON
L2M 5V6

Published by Crabtree Publishing in 2014

Author: Mary Colson
Editor: Shirley Duke
Proofreader: Anastasia Suen
Design concept: Lisa Peacock
Cover design: Samara Parent
Production coordinator and
    prepress technician: Ken Wright
Print coordinator: Margaret Amy Salter

First published in 2013 by Wayland
Copyright © Wayland 2013
(A division of Hachette Children's Books)
Produced for Wayland by Calcium

Printed in Canada/042016/BF20160217

Photographs:
Interior: Carbonfund.org: 33t; Dreamstime: 13, 86ccyy 22, Americanspirit 28b, Piero Cruciatti 23t, Hou Guima 27t, Himiko2023909 34b, Hsc 31, 38, Huating 25b, 26, Logit 2, 7tr, 17t, 17b, 24, Pavel Losevsky 34t, Hugo Maes 23b, Bartlomiej Magierowski 20, Pumba1 43t, Huguette Roe 30, Springdt313 39, Thisisdon 27m, Lukasz Tymszan 37, Zhanglianxun 25t; Shutterstock: 06photo 42, anaken2012 32t, Guryanov Andrey 8t, Yuri Arcurs 8b, Darren Baker 5b, beboy 33m, Dmitry Berkut 40, Ajay Bhaskar 7b, CJimenez 18t, dotshock 43b, Barone Firenze 44, Fotocrisis 6b, 10, hacohob 29, Pablo Hidalgo 11b,, hxdbzxy 15t, Jan S. 12,, Konstantin L 7t, lightpoet 45, Alberto Loyo 36, Bartlomiej Magierowski 15b, Oleksiy Mark 21, mikeledray 33b, Monkey Business Images 4, paintings 41, pio3 9, Pressmaster 5t, Huguette Roe 28t, soulgems 14, George Spade 7tl, 11t, Vlasov Volodymyr 18b, Vydrin 16, wavebreakmedia 19, 35, Feng Yu 32b.

Cover: wrangler/Shutterstock (top); Guryanov Andrey/Shutterstock (bottom left); Bartlomiej Magierowski/Dreamstime (bottom right)

Library and Archives Canada Cataloguing in Publication

Colson, Mary, author
    The true cost of technology / Mary Colson.

(Consumer nation : how to shop to change the world)
Includes index.
Issued in print and electronic formats.
ISBN 978-0-7787-0485-0 (bound).--ISBN 978-0-7787-0489-8 (pbk.).--
ISBN 978-1-4271-8210-4 (html).--ISBN 978-1-4271-8214-2 (pdf)

    1. Technology--Economic aspects--Juvenile literature.
2. Computer engineering--Juvenile literature. I. Title.

HC79.T4C65 2014   j338'.064   C2014-900373-0
                                            C2014-900374-9

Library of Congress Cataloging-in-Publication Data

Colson, Mary.
 The true cost of technology / Mary Colson.
     pages cm. -- (Consumer nation : how to shop to change the world)
 Includes index.
 ISBN 978-0-7787-0485-0 (reinforced library binding : alk. paper)
-- ISBN 978-0-7787-0489-8 (pbk. : alk. paper) -- ISBN 978-1-4271-8210-4 (electronic html : alk. paper) -- ISBN 978-1-4271-8214-2 (electronic pdf : alk. paper)
 1. Electronic industries--Social aspects--Juvenile literature. 2. Cost--Juvenile literature. 3. Externalities (Economics)--Juvenile literature. 4. Consumption (Economics)--Moral and ethical aspects--Juvenile literature. I. Title.

HD9696.A2C62 2014
338.4'76213--dc23
                                            2014002272

CONTENTS

Purchasing power...4
Techno-world map..6

Chapter 1 - World wide web........................8
Raw materials..10
Sweatshops: Human factories.....................12
The supply chain..14
Replacing people?...16

Chapter 2 - Working people.....................18
CASE STUDY 1: Computer children...............20
Working women's rights.................................22
CASE STUDY 2: Eat, work, sleep: life in a sweatshop compound...........24
Migrant workers...26

Chapter 3 - Waste matters.......................28
Designed to dump?..30
Eco-electronics..32

Chapter 4 - Techno-addicts......................34
CASE STUDY 3: Living online 24/7.................36
High-tech health matters..............................38

Chapter 5 - Campaigning for change.....40
Small steps to big change.............................42
Shop to change the world..............................44

Glossary...46
For more information.......................................47
Index...48

PURCHASING POWER

When you shop for a cool new phone, do you think about how your purchase might affect people elsewhere in the world? Do you ever wonder where your must-have video game systems come from? Would you buy your shiny new computer if you knew the keypad was made by child workers in China?

SHOP TO CHANGE THE WORLD

The electronics you buy and the money you spend affect people elsewhere. There's a vast global network or **supply chain** to ensure that the products you want are in the stores.

World wide web

The information technology (IT) and electronics industry is a global giant - the fastest growing business on the planet. All over the **developed world**, there is high **consumer** demand for computers, cell phones, and electronic games. In order to feed this greed for the latest technology, there is a human and an environmental cost.

The **United Nations (UN)** estimates that we replace our phones every 18 months and that only 0.5% of them are recycled. The rest go to **landfills**. There, along with unwanted game systems, old computer towers, and broken monitors, they leak poisonous lead and mercury into the **water supply**.

Today, techno-gadgets are central to many people's lives. How important are they to yours?

Going overseas

Many large western companies get their products made overseas where people's wages are low. This means the company makes more profit. If the products were made in the U.S., where wages are higher, the company would make much less profit.

Most offices today function with electronics like computers, printers, and telephones.

Factory conditions

Many technology factories are in China, Central America, and Asia, where the laws are very different. The workers live and work long hours in poor conditions and receive very little pay. Factories like these are called **sweatshops**.

People power

Computers, phones, and game systems look very clean and shiny, but is that the whole picture? This book looks at the links between the technology we buy and use in our daily lives and where it comes from. It will examine the links between supply, demand, labor conditions, resources, and waste. It will also look at **ethical shopping** and how things are improving. It will explain that you can shop to change the world.

SUPPLY AND DEMAND

China is the world's largest producer of electronic items. Over 1.3 million people work in Chinese computer cities where all the factories make products for American and European companies.

Family time is often spent playing computer and video games together.

5

TECHNO-WORLD MAP

- Over 75% of U.S. homes have a computer.

- Canadians lead the world in time spent on the Internet—an average of 45 hours per month.

- Sweden is the most technologically advanced country on Earth. Most people have access to Internet and cell phone reception. They live technology-based lives.

- The U.S. uses more energy per person per year than any other country on the planet.

- Around 77% of households in England have Internet access.

- The African country of Niger has the lowest number of computers per household in the world. Fewer than 1 in a 1,000 homes has a personal computer.

- Silver and tin are mined in Peru and Mexico.

- Tantalum is mined in the Democratic Republic of Congo.

- Copper is mined in Chile.

- Platinum for a hard drive comes from South Africa.

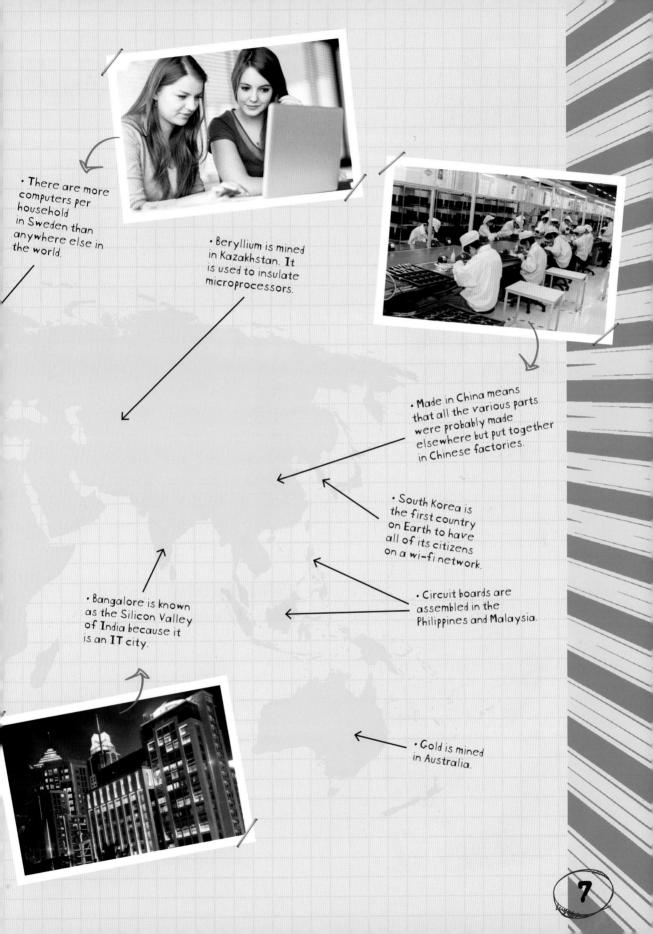

• There are more computers per household in Sweden than anywhere else in the world.

• Beryllium is mined in Kazakhstan. It is used to insulate microprocessors.

• Made in China means that all the various parts were probably made elsewhere but put together in Chinese factories.

• South Korea is the first country on Earth to have all of its citizens on a wi-fi network.

• Bangalore is known as the Silicon Valley of India because it is an IT city.

• Circuit boards are assembled in the Philippines and Malaysia.

• Gold is mined in Australia.

CHAPTER 1

WORLD WIDE WEB

When you buy a product in a store and take it home, it is the end of a long chain. Your computer, cell phone, or game system began life a long time before you owned it. This chapter will look at the supply chain of technology products from the resources used to make the products to the factory conditions of the assembly line and the journey to your door.

Young people are technology experts and want the latest products.

Supply chain

The supply chain is the process of how a product has its parts obtained, is made, and transported to the stores before you buy it and take it home. The plastic used to make your console might come from the oil fields of the Persian Gulf. The silicon chip inside your computer might come from the U.S., the screen may be produced in Japan, and the whole thing might be assembled in a factory in China. The product will then be packaged with cardboard, possibly made in Canada, shipped, and some months later, it might finally be bought by you.

Modern computer stores are high-tech in design as well as in the products they sell.

Being informed

It's easy to be a super-consumer. Before you buy, you could do an online search about the product and the company. This will tell you their track record in regard to working conditions at their factories, how they treat their workers, and whether they are concerned about the environment. You can also write or email the company and ask them about how they make their technology products. Having this information can help you make decisions about your purchases.

SHOP TO CHANGE THE WORLD

When you buy things in a store, you are called a consumer. You decide and choose what you consume. The labels on the box will tell you where a product is made. It will also give you information about who made it and whether the product uses recycled materials or is eco-friendly. The best labels will also tell you how to safely dispose of or recycle the item once you've finished with it. (See page 47 for details of electronics recycling.)

RAW MATERIALS

More than 130 million computers are produced every year around the world. With these huge numbers comes an enormous need for raw materials and energy. Making a computer and a screen takes around 530 pounds (240 kilograms) of fossil fuels, 46 lbs. (21 kg) of chemicals, and over 343 gallons (1,298 liters) of water. This is more than the weight of a car in resources for each computer.

Computer construction

Have you ever thought about what you need to make a computer? To begin with, you need plastic for the keyboard, glass for the screen, and metal for the key springs. But what else do you need?

Some technology products need over 1,000 different materials to make them. This means removing resources from the ground and processing them, resulting in a high environmental cost.

Copper mining in Chile creates sulfuric acid as a waste product. This is toxic to humans, wildlife, and water sources.

Recipe for a computer

You won't have room in your shopping cart for everything, so just get the basics. Most of them are available from oil fields, industrial mines, processing plants, and chemical factories.

Large-scale oil drilling feeds the technology industry's need for resources.

Material	Computer use?	Eco-impact?
Plastic	Computer casing, keyboard, and keys	High energy use to extract oil
Silicon	Screen, computer chip	Poisonous carbon monoxide is created during the ore processing phase
Copper	Wires, computer chip, and circuit board	Waste products become toxic to the environment; high water and energy use
Platinum	Hard drive	Very high energy use to mine; water pollution, toxic waste
Lead	Screen	Air pollution, toxic waste
Tin	USB ports	Destruction of forests and coral reefs in some tin mining nations
Aluminum	Absorb heat and keep computer cool	Mining process creates carbon dioxide, which is toxic in large amounts
Mercury	Switches	Water pollution, highly toxic
Cadmium	Battery	Highly toxic, air pollution
PVC (Polyvinyl Chloride)	Casing for computer cables and circuit boards	Poisons the air where it is burned

SUPPLY AND DEMAND

The world's largest copper mine is in the Atacama Desert in South America, the driest place on Earth. Up to 721 gallons (2,729 liters) of water per second are required to extract copper so large **desalination plants** purify sea water that is pumped across the desert. Sulphuric acid is a **toxic** waste product of this process and it needs to be disposed of very carefully.

Silicon and copper are used to make these silicon chips, the basic element of all computers.

SWEATSHOPS: HUMAN FACTORIES

Once the resources have been removed, processed, and used to make the parts required, the products must be assembled. This next step in the supply chain is sometimes done by machines, but because of the small parts, a lot of the products in the **IT** and technology industries are assembled by people.

SUPPLY AND DEMAND

It is estimated that 85% of sweatshop workers are between 15 and 25 years old. They work 60–80 hours per week and sometimes receive only pennies for their work. They have to spend 50–75% of their income on food because their pay is so low.

Consumer demand

In industrialized countries, while meeting the demand for cheaper products, companies look for ways to cut costs so that their profits stay high. In order to do this they often set up factories overseas where people are paid less. Some of the workers in these factories experience terrible conditions. These factories, known as sweatshops, are an unfortunate part of the global business chain called supply and demand.

Child labor

The cheapest workers of all are children and some sweatshops employ hundreds of underage laborers. Many of the children must work to help their parents, who are not paid enough to provide for the family. An education is out of the question for these children, who have to work instead of going to school.

Living standards for sweatshop workers in some countries can be very low. The poorest people live in slums like this one in Mumbai, India.

A life of labor

The working conditions in sweatshops are often very poor or even unsafe. Workers are forced to work overtime, made to work in dangerous and unhealthy environments, and threatened if they complain. They may also have to handle toxic chemical paints, **solvents**, and glues with their bare hands in closed rooms with no fresh air.

Global shame

Sweatshops exist all over the world, from Central and South America to Asia and certain regions of Europe. There are even sweatshops in New York, San Francisco, and Los Angeles.

SHOP TO CHANGE THE WORLD

Fair trade means paying workers a fair wage for their work. There is a special logo that all fair trade products have on their packaging. Sometimes, they cost a little bit more, but it does mean that they are made in factories where people work in good conditions. It makes the supply chain fairer for everyone.

In this factory in Shenzhen, China, workers make component parts for closed-circuit television (CCTV) cameras.

THE SUPPLY CHAIN

The primary purpose of any business is to make money. The technology industry is so international and competitive that businesses will do their best to keep on top. This flow chart explains how the raw materials, factories, and workers can all play their part in keeping **manufacturing costs** down and maximizing profit.

1. A technology company in a developed country like the U.S. wants to make computers, mobile phones, and gaming systems. There's lots of competition from other companies, and consumers want cheap goods so...

2. ... they gather the raw materials required from dozens of different sources and companies all over the world. They drive a hard bargain and get the materials as cheaply as possible.

Modern office buildings can often hide the grim realities of the supply chain.

7. The American company pays a different company to manage the factory operations and make the products.

8. The workers live and work at the factories. They assemble high-tech electronics for less than a dollar an hour and work up to 80 hours per week. They can get fired without any notice and rarely have a day off.

9. The technology company owners probably never see the factory so they can turn a blind eye and ignore the working conditions.

In Asia, there are many overcrowded cities with large numbers of people looking for jobs.

3. American labor costs are too high so the company uses factories in developing countries, such as China, Taiwan, or the Philippines, where wages are much lower. This is called **outsourcing**.

4. The governments of these developing countries are pleased to have American money being invested and to have lots of jobs being created.

6. The employment agency gives unemployed people work in the factories for a fee. The workers then spend months paying this off before they make any money themselves.

5. The technology company employs another company or employment agency to hire workers.

10. The finished product is packaged, shipped, and sold all over the world with as little cost and as much profit as possible.

Workers on an assembly line spend many hours at their workstation.

End of the line?

Whether it's a cherished smartphone, tablet, or games system, the technology was probably made and assembled in Asia by workers who have few rights and often toil under sweatshop-like conditions. Who do you think is responsible for keeping things like this and what can be done to change the situation?

REPLACING PEOPLE?

When you think of a high-tech factory, what do you picture? Do you see people in white overalls operating space-age machinery in clean white rooms? Or do you see row upon row of low-paid workers picking computer chips off a conveyor belt in a dark and dingy warehouse? Whatever you imagine, you probably have only part of the picture.

Robot world

Many technology companies are taking the step from a human workforce to a robot one. Some companies who have been using sweatshop labor have invested in robots. The company can maximize their profits without forcing people to work in bad conditions. Do you think this is a step in the right direction? Is this the answer to poor factory conditions? What about people's jobs?

Is this a vision of the future? Could all technology factories replace people with robots?

In this factory in China, workers are given protective clothing and face masks so they don't inhale chemicals.

Uniting for change

Not every company is going super-high tech and workers in some factories are getting together to lobby for change. By protesting and going on strike, the workers hope to let people know about their harsh working conditions and raise awareness of their situation. They are starting to stand up for their **human rights**. They want their bosses to make positive changes, not simply replace them with robots.

What's a union?

A union is a special group that represents people's opinions or their professional interests. It might be a group of teachers or nurses or factory workers who are seeking improvements at work or in their pay. Having a few key people to speak up on behalf of many is an effective way to get issues and feelings raised. Union leaders meet with bosses or government officials who can make changes happen.

CONSUMER NATION

What are the pros and cons of using robots instead of workers?

Pros
1. Robots don't need to be paid
2. They won't go on strike
3. They can work all day long, without needing a break

Cons
1. Millions of people become unemployed
2. 'Computer cities' turn into ghost towns with mass **poverty**
3. The human sweatshop problem simply moves to a place where wages are even lower

2

WORKING PEOPLE

Think about what you use a computer and your phone for. Games? Email? Contacting friends? Now, think about what your parents use them for. It's likely that they rely on them for quite a lot of their daily lives, from ordering groceries and finding out what's on in the area, to checking their bank account. This equipment is amazing and we would find it hard to live without it, but there is a cost to our technology. This chapter looks at the different people, often many thousands of miles away, who are paying the price.

Working life

You've probably heard your mom or dad come home and complain about work sometimes. Maybe they're tired or they've had a bad or busy day. This happens to everybody sometimes, but not every day. The electronics industry is one of the worst businesses for ensuring good quality work spaces for its employees, especially during manufacture and assembly.

Go http://www

Surfing the Internet is part of everyday life. Can you imagine your day without it?

Research and development

When a business develops a new product, such as a tablet or smartphone, it takes many years of work to perfect it. There's a lot of trial and error and sometimes a company will spend millions of dollars before abandoning the project altogether. Even for the successful products, there is a huge investment of time and money before it ever gets to the stores, so businesses try to get back some of that money in the manufacturing and price. It might only cost $82 to make a computer if it's made somewhere like China, where the salaries are low. However, we pay a lot more to cover the years of product development.

Many students rely on technology like tablets and computers to access the Internet and look up information.

SHOP TO CHANGE THE WORLD

It's important to think before you buy, so as you read through this chapter, ask yourself the following questions:
1. Should more money be spent on the workers?
2. If it were, would that improve conditions?
3. Is more money always the answer?
4. What could businesses do to change things?
5. What could you and your family do to change things?
Talk about your answers with your mom or dad and think about who you believe is responsible for how things are. How could you help change things?

CASE STUDY 1
COMPUTER CHILDREN

Children all over the world enjoy playing on their computers, phones and games consoles. It can help their social skills and their coordination, and it's a part of modern childhood. But there are some computer children who never get to play with any of the gadgets we now take for granted: they are the forgotten workers in the technology chain.

Overworked, underpaid, and overlooked

See for yourself. Products for a technology company are made in this factory in China. There are wooden benches on either side of a slow-moving conveyor belt carrying webcams. The benches are full of workers. Some of the workers look very young. Chen is 14 years old.

Like all the child workers, Chen has to stand up during his shift, which can last up to 15 hours. He can also be told to work overtime on top of this. His pay is so low that he earns less than a dollar an hour.

CCD VIDEO CAMERA

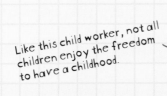
Like this child worker, not all children enjoy the freedom to have a childhood.

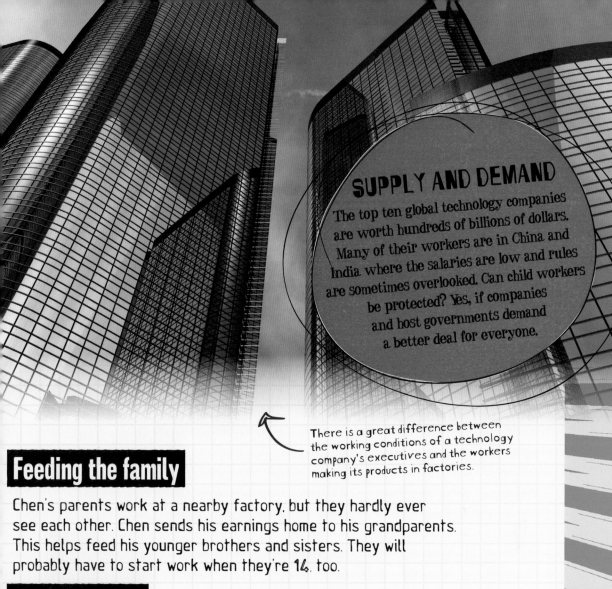

SUPPLY AND DEMAND

The top ten global technology companies are worth hundreds of billions of dollars. Many of their workers are in China and India where the salaries are low and rules are sometimes overlooked. Can child workers be protected? Yes, if companies and host governments demand a better deal for everyone.

There is a great difference between the working conditions of a technology company's executives and the workers making its products in factories.

Feeding the family

Chen's parents work at a nearby factory, but they hardly ever see each other. Chen sends his earnings home to his grandparents. This helps feed his younger brothers and sisters. They will probably have to start work when they're 14, too.

Lost childhood

Chen misses out on many things, but mostly he's missed out on a childhood. Chen hasn't gone to school and he doesn't have free time. Because his parents aren't there, he has no one to talk to about his problems. He misses his parents but he has to work to help the family.

Child protection

The International Labour Organization (ILO) has made June 12th the World Day Against Child Labor. This day helps raise awareness of the suffering of child workers like Chen around the world. The ILO has a legal code which states that child labor must be **outlawed** and that there must be a minimum age for employment. This minimum should not be below the age for completing the required schooling.

WORKING WOMEN'S RIGHTS

Millions of workers, most of them women, work in tens of thousands of sweatshops around the world. Labor advocate groups estimate that 85% of sweatshop workers are young women between the ages of 15-25.

Many of the workers in Chinese technology factories are women. They often go to work in order to pay for a better education for their children. But this comes at a high price to both their health and their family life.

Paid slaves

The salaries that most women are paid in sweatshops won't give them a basic standard of living. Young women are often drawn into work by employment agents promising them good pay in another country. The women pay the agents, who give them contracts to sign. The contracts say that the women workers have to pay money each month to the agents. They can be paying for years because there are no controls over the dishonest agents.

A female factory worker in China may not have as many rights as female workers in other parts of the world.

Harsh choice

Some women in Central American and Mexican factories live in fear of being fired if they become pregnant. There is little chance of finding another job as a pregnant woman and there is no **maternity pay**. Many female workers put up with awful conditions without complaining. Unions are banned in many countries so the workers don't even have the chance to express their views.

In some factories, like this one in China, the equipment is often old and the workstations poorly lit.

Changing times?

The UN and human rights organizations, such as Amnesty International, are working to improve conditions for women in employment around the world. If you want to get involved, check out the anti-slavery movements on their websites.

Some factories provide better conditions, but the pay may still be very low.

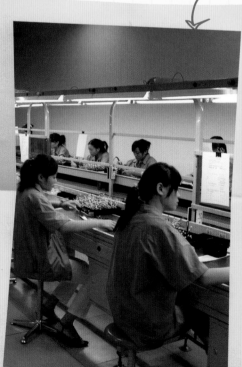

CONSUMER NATION

Do you think it's a good idea to employ women in developing countries?

Pros

1. By allowing women to earn their own money, they are more in control of their lives and not reliant on others.
2. Both parents should contribute to a family's income, not just the father.
3. The more skilled the whole workforce is, the better it is for a country.

Cons

1. If women work, they are unable to be a full-time mother.
2. If workers become pregnant, employers may think it's a waste of their job training.
3. Children need at least one parent at home to be a role model.

CASE STUDY 2

EAT, WORK, SLEEP: LIFE IN A SWEATSHOP COMPOUND

Imagine a job advertisement that promises food and housing on top of your pay. Sounds good, doesn't it? Yet, things aren't always what they seem.

Computer factory, Zhongguancun, Beijing, China

It's 7pm. Bai has been sitting on his hard wooden stool in his place on the assembly line for nearly 12 hours. It's Sunday. He hasn't had a day off for over three weeks. His eyes are starting to close with tiredness and he rubs them to keep awake. *Click.* Yawning, he picks up another keyboard key and clicks it into place. *Click.* He knows the QWERTY keyboard by heart now. *Click.* He can't read or speak English and he's never used a computer, but he knows the QWERTY keyboard by heart. *Click.*

Every second counts

Around 500 computer keyboards an hour move down the assembly line, one every 7.2 seconds. Like his co-workers, Bai has just 1.1 seconds to snap and click each key into place. He will repeat this action 3,250 times every hour. That's 35,750 times a day, 250,250 times a week, and over one million times a month.

Workers on an assembly line in a factory producing laptop computers in China. Assembly line work is extremely repetitive and pressure-filled.

All Bai thinks is that every hour, he's earned another 54 cents to send home to help feed his family. *Click.* He reaches for another keyboard key. *Click.* He needs to go to the restroom, but he knows he's not allowed to go during shifts. *Click.*

Far-away family

Bai is just one of over two thousand workers in this factory. He's been on keyboards since he arrived in the city from the countryside six months ago. His home town and family are over 124 miles (200 km) away. He hasn't been back once. He's had two days off each month since he arrived, but he had to spend most of those days lining up to make a ten-minute phone call home. He's hoping to travel home for three days at the end of the year.

Factory workers on assembly lines work at high speed for hours.

The better factory compounds have recreation areas for the workers to use when they're not on their shift.

Day's end

Bai's shift comes to an end. With a final click of the last keyboard key in place, he stands and stretches. Before he has walked ten steps toward the door, another worker has taken his place. The factory never stops.

After some noodle soup in the cafeteria, Bai returns to his dormitory. Twelve workers share a room. They bathe with hot water from a bucket. Bai sits on his narrow metal bed. His whole body aches with tiredness. He lies down and reaches for the light switch. *Click.*

MIGRANT WORKERS

Guangdong Province, China, is a vast region of farmland, remote villages, and small, close-knit communities. The crops have failed again and there's no work. Many of the young men and women from the village will have to leave and find work in the cities.

Many miles away, the city welcomes new arrivals from the countryside every day. Hundreds arrive each week. Carrying their bags of belongings, they search for a job. They don't know when they'll see their families again, but it's their only chance to make a living. This is the grim reality facing tens of thousands of **migrant workers** in China.

Dream job?

The technology industry thrives in the cities of Guangdong Province. Signs on factories boast of good working conditions and decent pay. But once inside, the workers are put to work right away on assembly lines. It's not such a dream job after all.

SUPPLY AND DEMAND

The majority of the workers in computer factories are young, single, migrant workers between the ages of 16 and 25 years old. Their official papers show that they are registered as country people. This means that they can be let go and sent back as soon as the demand for products goes down. No matter how long they have been working in the city, they are not permitted to stay there permanently.

Company buses pick up workers to take them to a factory in Zhuhai, China.

This chemical factory in Beijing bellows polluting smoke into the city's skyline. It is a similar sight in many cities throughout China.

Desperate people leave their homes and move to cities, such as Guangzhou, looking for work. Those who don't find a job may end up begging on the streets.

No protection

If the workers want to get married, the factory owners reduce their pay instead of giving them a yearly vacation. If a female worker has a child, the schooling of that child is the responsibility of the worker's home community, as far as the owners are concerned. If the worker has an accident and suffers a serious injury, there is no cash support from the factory owners. Injured workers have to return to their home village to be looked after. There is no sick pay or **disability benefit** from the government.

Who's to blame?

What do you think? Is it the fault of the factory owners? Or should the technology companies check factory conditions more? What about us? Should we change our buying habits?

CHAPTER 3

WASTE MATTERS

When your computer or cell phone has started to slow down or you want to upgrade to the latest model, what do you do with it? Where does it go? The technology we use to manage our lives fuels a need for more power, and that has consequences, too. This chapter looks at the issues surrounding electronic waste, along with its impact on the environment and human health.

Sorting through technology waste can be dangerous for workers if they don't wear protective clothing.

Poison power?

Phones, laptops, and games systems all use remote controls that run on different kinds of batteries. Batteries contain at least eight toxic metals, including cadmium, lead, zinc, manganese, nickel, mercury, silver, and lithium. They also contain acids. While they are being used, they are safe. The problems come once the batteries are dead. If batteries are thrown away into a normal landfill site, they can start to leak their toxic chemicals into the groundwater. Mercury batteries are gradually being phased out, but all the metals contained in batteries are harmful to humans if they get into our food chain.

High energy use

All our electronics are energy-greedy. Whether they are plugged into the outlets or use batteries, our technology tools have a constant demand for power.

The more electricity we require, the more needs to be produced. In the U.S., electricity comes from coal-fired generators, which pollute the air with carbon dioxide. Natural gas is burned to run generators, and this fossil fuel adds carbon dioxide as well.

An average computer uses 200 watts per hour. Over a year, this is 584,000 watts of energy that must be generated. This is around four times the amount of energy a lightbulb uses, and it would power over 500 toasters.

Electric equality?

The average household in the U.S. uses 11,280 kilowatts hours of electricity per year. This is over one-third of the total energy going to run our homes and appliances in it. The U.S. has about 5% of the world's population but uses almost 25% of the world's total energy—the most of any country. This isn't sustainable for the planet.

SUPPLY AND DEMAND

The more our lives depend on technology, the more energy we need to power these devices. Did you know that we use the most energy when we leave our electronics on standby? Leaving appliances on standby rather than turning them off makes up to 5 to 10% of household energy use. That's about $1,354 per family in the U.S., or $155 billion nationwide.

DESIGNED TO DUMP?

Electronic waste is the fastest growing sector of household and business waste and it all needs to go somewhere. Many local governments have recycling centers where electronic goods can be taken and then processed, but what does processed mean? And are manufacturers doing anything to make all our high-tech electronics less throwaway?

Enormous amounts of e-waste

E-waste is the fastest growing part of our trash. More than 1.1 million tons (1 million metric tons) a year needs to be dealt with. It's estimated that around 40% of lead and 75% of other heavy metals like cadmium and mercury found in U.S. landfills comes from discarded electronic equipment. Global e-waste is more than 55 million tons (50 million metric tons) and only 10% is recycled.

E-waste mountains are growing fast as we update and replace our high-tech electronics.

The developed world has an unquenchable thirst for circuit boards for new high-tech electronics.

SUPPLY AND DEMAND

Did you know that 40–50% of the environmental impact of a mobile phone occurs as its wiring boards and circuits are being made? After purchase, the average user then replaces their cell phone every 11 to 18 months. The discarded phones then contribute to the e-waste mountain.

Hiding the problem

Much of our e-waste, including old computer monitors, televisions, game systems, and cell phones, isn't recycled in this country but shipped overseas. E-waste from the U.S. and Europe is sent to India and other Asian and African countries. Governments pay to store their waste in these countries with developing economies. The problem is the waste isn't sorted properly or made safe first, so much of it is toxic.

Health hazard

When televisions, cell phones, and computer processors are broken down, lead, mercury, and other chemicals are released into the air and water sources, causing pollution. In poor countries, workers don't have protective clothing and there are few, if any, health and safety regulations. Once these chemicals get into drinking wells, people can develop serious illnesses, such as cancer.

SHOP TO CHANGE THE WORLD

Various **advocate groups**, such as Ethical Consumer, are working for industry changes. They want manufacturers to be responsible for removing harmful chemicals from their products and for safely recycling or disposing of their electronics.

31

ECO-ELECTRONICS

Some technology firms are starting to sit up and take notice of the environment and the problems that the supply chain creates. Companies such as IBM abide by a code pledging not to use sweatshops and not to pollute. Organizations such as United Pepper locate electronics made by ethical companies and then sell them online. Bamboo plastic casings for tablet and low energy-use screens are part of a new wave of products on the market.

SHOP TO CHANGE THE WORLD

How can you measure a company in terms of its environmental record, human rights and fair pay? There are many advocate groups and organizations such as Better World Shopper that focus on finding out this important information. They use dozens of different data sources and company reports to arrive at their conclusions and rankings. If a company finds itself ranked in the top ten worst companies, it might be forced to change its bad business practices because it doesn't want bad publicity. (For more details, see page 47.)

The lithium used in batteries for personal computers (PC), cameras, and cell phones is highly toxic and must be disposed of safely.

PCs don't have to go out of date. They can be upgraded rather than replaced.

Eco-labels

Across the world, there are many different labels and logos for products that are more eco-friendly or ethical to help you when you're shopping. International examples include the BEST logo, which represents low lead use in batteries, and the CarbonFree label, which is on products made with very low **greenhouse gas** emissions. Earthsure and Energy Star are other labels on products that show good environmental awareness, while the SEE (what you are buying) label is on products which avoid sweatshops.

Top tips for techno-trash!

Many organizations suggest the following ways to recycle or re-use your old electronics:

1. Donate for reuse if possible.
2. Find a recycler near you.
3. See if the manufacturer has a free recycling program.
4. Find out which stores in your area will take old PCs.
5. Lots of companies offer money back in exchange for old phones. If you upgrade, they can safely dispose of your old one.
6. Recycle rechargeable batteries.
7. Use Freecycle or another community recycling program.

SAVE THE EARTH RECYCLE

Remember to recycle your high-tech products and you'll be a super-consumer!

CHAPTER 4

TECHNO-ADDICTS

How much of your life is dependent on modern technology? How many hours a day do you spend online or gaming? How many text messages do you send each day? Could you live without these tech-tools? Are you a techno-addict?

Connecting people

The UN has reported that cell phones are spreading faster than any other technology. They're changing how we communicate with each other and how we live. They've become an extension of our hands and our minds—almost an essential part of us. Many Americans see their cell phone as their best friend and are lost without it. Have we become addicted to our phones?

Computer games are great fun but sometimes people spend too much of their time playing them.

Crazy for games

The gaming industry is a powerful and influential one. Games are an important part of many people's free time and a way they relax. All over the world, children and adults alike are gripped by Nintendos, Wiis, X-boxes, Play Stations, and other gaming devices. You can become a different character, explore other worlds, and be a virtual hero. But what lies behind the pretty pictures, superhero actions, and sense of power the player has?

Game addiction is a very real issue many people are facing today. Spending hours and hours alone in a virtual world, they find it hard to cope when they log off and have to interact with people in the normal world. This can lead to family arguments, anti-social behavior, and in the case of young people, sleep and schoolwork being badly affected.

SUPPLY AND DEMAND

In 2009, the first U.S. rehabilitation center for video game addiction opened. It is estimated that 8.5% of American youth show signs of video game addictive behavior. That is almost one in ten people who play video games. The key to living with technology safely is to enjoy it without letting it rule you.

Game addiction can make it hard to concentrate on everyday activities, such as school.

CONSUMER NATION

Are you for or against computer games?

Pros

1 They can help to improve your coordination skills.

2. They may encourage your imagination.

3. You feel a sense of achievement when you do well.

Cons

1 You spend a lot of time alone with imaginary characters rather than talking to or playing with your real friends.

2. You find it hard to sleep so you're always tired.

3. You stay indoors and may exercise less.

CASE STUDY 3
LIVING ONLINE 24/7

Many high-tech IT companies have set up **virtual sweatshops** in Eastern Europe and parts of Asia. These are where young gamers are paid to play games for other people. It may seem like the ideal job, being paid to game 24/7. It's part of a global industry worth billions of dollars. You might think that if the people are being paid a fair local salary, then what's the problem?

Staring at a screen

Picture a drafty, run-down apartment block in India. In one of the apartments on the fourth floor, there are rows of tables and chairs. A small kitchen has a teapot and some dirty cups. There are no pictures on the walls. On the chairs, sit a dozen young people staring at computer screens and furiously hitting keys. They don't blink, they don't talk: they just play.

Virtual sweatshops may be set up in an apartment block such as this one in India.

Changeover

It's 7p.m. as Raj arrives at the apartment. He has come here most days for the past seven months. He's trying to pay his way through college by working the night shift. He nods to one or two of the other gamers and then takes the seat of Adil, a day shift worker.

Round the clock

Among them, 12 employees play day and night, seven days a week. A U.S. company pays for the apartment, the computers, and the workers' salaries of around $115 per month. Sometimes, Raj and his colleagues are testing new games and sometimes they are paid to play on behalf of wealthy players when they themselves are at work or asleep.

Paying for play

There are hundreds of computer games for which millions of people pay a monthly fee to keep their characters in the game. For the workers like Raj, who play for others, the games can be highly addictive. Sometimes, Raj comes in on his day off just to continue playing. His courses are suffering and he hasn't slept well in weeks. He doesn't talk to his family much. He hasn't got the energy or the time to find another job; he was lucky to get this one. He just can't stop playing...

Complicated problems like these aren't easy to solve, but what ideas do you have? What rules would you put in place to stop people becoming addicted to gaming, and what help would you provide for addicts?

HIGH-TECH HEALTH MATTERS

Imagine having to handle and inhale chemicals in your everyday work. What about having to look at a screen all day long? How would your eyes feel? Think about sitting at a desk for a few hours and then trying to stretch. Many stages of the technology production line involve activities that are potentially harmful to health.

Toxic technology

Did you know that behind your bright monitor is almost nine pounds (four kg) of lead? The health effects of lead are well known. Lead exposure causes brain damage in children and it has been banned from many consumer products.

Some monitors use lead and mercury lamps; some even use poisonous arsenic. Like lead, mercury is toxic in very low doses and causes brain and kidney damage. Just 1/70th of a teaspoon of mercury is enough to contaminate 20 acres of a lake, making the fish living in it unfit to eat. Lead dust in the air can be swallowed and passed on through breast milk.

The lead in computers can be harmful to both the factory workers and to the environment.

Risky business?

Millions of workers all over the world work in the technology industry, and many are exposed to harmful chemicals and practices. Indium and cadmium are two chemicals used in computers, and both of them can cause kidney problems. PVC fumes can also cause breathing difficulties if used in closed spaces. The U.N. is working for improvements to be made in the electronics and technology industries, but some damage has already been done.

Post-production problems

The problems aren't just in the manufacturing stages, though. A recent study of dust on computers in workplaces and homes found brominated flame retardants (BFRs) in every sample taken. BFRs are used in electronic products as a way of protecting against fire. BFRs may seriously affect hormonal functions, which are vital for normal physical development. Alarming rates of BFRs have been found in the breast milk of women in the U.S. and Sweden.

SHOP TO CHANGE THE WORLD

You can play your part in helping make the electronics industry cleaner, greener, and healthier by buying products from companies that don't use harmful chemicals. Dell, Hewlett Packard, Nokia, Samsung and Sony have made a commitment to phase out hazardous chemicals. This will make each stage of the manufacturing and disposal safer and more eco-friendly.

Ethical companies, such as this one in Shanghai, China, make sure their workers are well protected from harmful substances.

CHAPTER 5

CAMPAIGNING FOR CHANGE

There are many influential organizations and groups who are making a difference to the way the technology industry operates. They take actions to make things better for workers, avoid exploiting children, and improve the environmental impact of our technology.

SUPPLY AND DEMAND

The more demand there is for a product, the more money a company will make from selling it. Advocate groups work in the same way. The more people they represent, the more a company will listen to them. If they can supply voices of protest, then they can demand change.

Putting on the pressure

Advocate groups work to make a difference through their actions. They target and meet with individual companies and governments in order to do this. Sometimes, they conduct undercover investigations and embarrass the businesses with their findings and the resulting publicity. A business will probably change its practices if they are worried about customers going elsewhere.

Group power

UNICEF (United Nations Children's Fund) is a U.N. agency looking after children's rights. The charity Save the Children also advocates against child labor. Pressure from the group, Make IT Fair has also caused some technology companies to change their ways for the better. These and other groups have online forms called **petitions** that you can sign to show your support for their causes.

Eco-awareness

Environmental groups, such as Greenpeace, Friends of the Earth, and Kids for Saving Earth, work to educate and bring about better use of Earth's resources. They are also concerned with the level of industrial pollution created by the technology industry. For more information, see page 47.

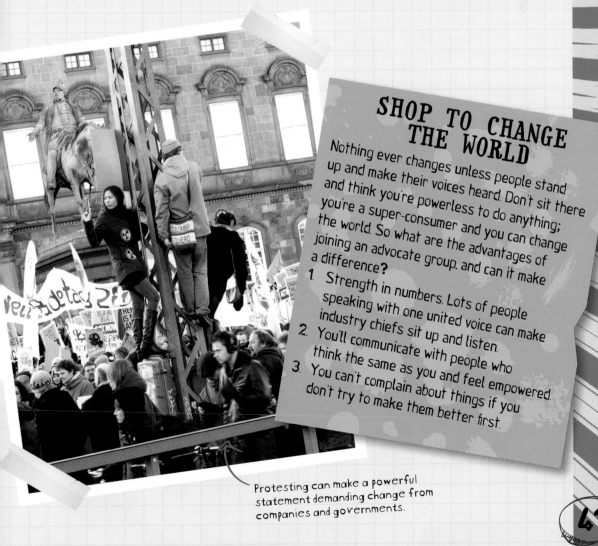

SHOP TO CHANGE THE WORLD

Nothing ever changes unless people stand up and make their voices heard. Don't sit there and think you're powerless to do anything; you're a super-consumer and you can change the world. So what are the advantages of joining an advocate group, and can it make a difference?

1. Strength in numbers. Lots of people speaking with one united voice can make industry chiefs sit up and listen.
2. You'll communicate with people who think the same as you and feel empowered.
3. You can't complain about things if you don't try to make them better first.

Protesting can make a powerful statement demanding change from companies and governments.

SMALL STEPS TO BIG CHANGE

In towns and cities all over the world, if you look carefully, you can see that small changes are happening. Some companies are making an effort to do things better and improve things along the supply chain for people and the planet.

SHOP TO CHANGE THE WORLD

We all like to be up to date and keep pace with our friends on the technology front, but what do you really need? It's important to understand technology and the advantages that electronics, games, and phones can give us, but remember, it's about being a sensible consumer and not just having more stuff.

Cooperation

Small-scale business communities all over the world are improving their own working conditions and supply chains. In some technology factories and mineral mines, workers are starting to unite and form unions. This makes it possible for their concerns to be heard. On a larger scale, governments are starting to sign international legal agreements concerning human rights and environmental protection.

This modern, well-lit factory puts its workers' safety first with the correct safety clothing and equipment.

Making a change

Many technology companies are owned by shareholders, meaning people who have bought shares in the company on the stock market. The shareholders can influence what the company does when they vote on certain decisions. The more money a shareholder has invested, the more power he or she has. Further along the supply chain, consumers have power, too. Finding out about how products are made, what eco-impact they have, and how the workers are treated can help us to make informed choices.

Perfect chain

It is possible to achieve a fair and eco-friendly supply chain in the technology industry, but it will take everyone involved to demand less and supply a little more in terms of time and money. For the sake of workers and the planet, companies and governments need to play by *all* the rules.

Take a look around, find out about the product and the company...

SUPPLY AND DEMAND

If your computer or phone is no longer working as fast or as well as you'd like, consider your options before you replace. You may be able to keep your keyboard or your tower and simply add more memory or a new battery. Remember, whatever you demand, businesses will supply—so don't let them encourage you to buy something new if you don't really need or want it.

... and make an informed choice when you buy. Encourage your family to do the same. That way, you'll really make a difference.

SHOP TO CHANGE THE WORLD

The making, selling, and buying chain of any product is complicated and usually involves many different people all over the world. Everything has a cost and it's not just the one on the box of your product. We as consumers and buyers play a key role in this chain.

Time for change?

There are many people and organizations who are responsible for keeping things the way they are, from companies wanting to make the most profit possible to consumers like us wanting low prices. At some point, someone in the chain is going to suffer if things continue to go on in this way.

Governments of developing countries welcome the investment and the jobs that technology factories bring, but they rarely check on the working conditions to make sure the workers are well looked after. We increasingly rely on high-tech electronics to organize our lives, but it's the sweatshop workers and the environment that really pay the price.

Technology companies spend huge amounts of money marketing their products to potential buyers. Consumers can use their spending power to help create a fairer industry.

The buck stops here!

As a consumer of technology tools, you have real power to change things. You are the end of the chain and if you're not happy with a product or how it's made, then companies will listen to you because they want you to buy their item. Fair trade means that shoppers can be responsible and demand fairness at all stages of the supply chain.

Today, many people buy only from companies that treat their employees and the environment well. You can avoid buying products by companies who use sweatshops, child labor, or have a poor environmental record. Our technology-based lives really shouldn't have to cost the Earth.

SUPPLY AND DEMAND

There are many programs launched to focus attention on working conditions in the electronics industry in developing countries. Clean up your computer is run by a charity demanding that sweatshop workers in the technology industry are treated according to international working standards.

Enjoy technology but don't let it rule your life!

SHOP TO CHANGE THE WORLD

You could join a group working to change conditions for technology factory workers for the better. You could also push for a reduction in toxic emissions. There are many online groups and lots of information out there. See page 47 for more details.

GLOSSARY

advocate groups   Organizations of people who put pressure on governments or companies to make changes

assembly   Putting different pieces together to make one product

consumer   A person who buys products to use

desalination plants   Factories where saltwater is changed to freshwater

developed world   Industrialized countries

disability benefit   Government money for disabled people who can't work

ethical shopping   Buying products from companies that have a good supply chain and fair conditions for workers

exploited   Taken advantage of

fair trade   Fairly sharing profits along the supply chain

fossil fuels   Fuels, such as coal, oil, and natural gas, that formed from the remains of ancient plants and animals

greenhouse gas   A gas that contributes to global warming, such as carbon dioxide and methane

human rights   The safety, security, and education that every person on Earth is entitled to

landfill   A place where garbage is dumped and covered with dirt

manufacturing costs   What it costs to make any product

maternity pay   A salary paid to women when they take time off work to have a baby

migrant workers   People who travel around seeking seasonal work

outlawed   Something that is banned or illegal

outsourcing   Buying labor or materials from elsewhere, usually because it is cheaper

petitions   Signed written requests for change

poverty   Not having enough money for basic needs such as food, clothing, or housing

rehabilitation center   A place where gaming addicts can go to receive medical help

solvents   Substances that dissolve other matter in them to form a solution

supply chain   All the people and materials that go into making and distributing a product

sweatshops   Factories with poor working conditions and low pay

toxic   Poisonous

UN   Stands for the United Nations, an international organization founded in 1945 to promote peace, security, and economic development

virtual sweatshops   Places of work with conditions like a factory sweatshop

water supply   Groundwater

FOR MORE INFORMATION

Books

Powell, Jillian. *Fair Trade (Explore)*. Wayland, 2014.

Hunt, Jilly. *Fair Trade (Hot Topics)*. Heinemann Library, 2012.

Sheth, Kashmira. *Boys Without Names*. HarperCollins, 2011.

Gleason, Carrie. *Environmental Activist (Get Involved!)*. Crabtree Publishing, 2010.

Rodger, Ellen. *Human Rights Activist (Get Involved!)*. Crabtree Publishing, 2010.

Bauman, Amy. *Natural Resources (Planet Earth)*. Tick Tock, 2008.

Websites

www.computerhope.com/disposal.htm
Find U.S. companies that collect, repair, and recycle old electronic equipment.

If you're interested in joining an advocate group or finding out more about being a super-consumer, check out the following websites:

www.dosomething.org
This is a great website for teenagers to get involved in issues you care about.

www.sweatfree.org/shopping
See what this charity is doing to assist sweatshop workers around the world.

www.betterworldshopper.org
This website rates companies on thier social and environmental responsibility.

www.greenpeace.org
Find out about environmental issues and what you can do to make a difference.

www.kidsforsavingearth.org
This website is all about how you can help to protect our planet.

INDEX

addiction 34-36, 37

advocate groups 31, 32, 40, 41

assembly line 8, 12, 14, 15, 18, 24, 25, 26

being a consumer 4, 9, 12, 14, 33, 41, 42, 43, 44, 45

business 4, 12, 14, 18, 19, 30, 32, 40, 42, 43

chemicals 10, 11, 13, 17, 27, 28, 31, 38, 39

child workers 4, 12, 20-21, 40, 41, 45

computers 4, 5, 6, 7, 8, 9, 10, 11, 13, 14, 15, 16, 17, 18, 19, 20, 24-25, 26, 31, 32, 34, 35, 36, 37, 38, 39, 45

developed world 4, 14, 31

developing world 15, 23, 29, 44, 45

e-waste 30-31

eco-friendly products 9, 32-33, 39, 43

electronic products 4, 5, 9, 18, 25, 28, 29, 30, 32-33, 39, 45

environment 4, 9, 10, 11, 28, 31, 32, 33, 38, 40, 41, 42, 43, 44, 45

factory conditions 5, 8, 16, 17, 18-19, 22-23, 24-25, 26, 27, 38, 42, 45

fair trade 13, 45

fossil fuels 8, 10, 11

games consoles 4, 5, 8, 14, 15, 20, 28, 31

human rights 17, 23, 32, 42

metals 10, 11, 28, 30

migrant workers 26-27

mobile phones 4, 5, 7, 8, 14, 28, 31, 34

money 4, 14, 15, 19, 21, 22, 23, 29, 33, 36, 37, 40, 43, 44

natural resources 5, 8, 10, 11, 12, 41

pay 12, 20, 22-23, 32

profit 5, 12, 14, 15, 16, 40, 44

raw materials 10-11, 14

recycling 4, 9, 30, 31, 33

silicon chip 8, 11

supply chain 4, 5, 8, 12, 13, 14-15, 32, 42, 43, 45

sweatshop workers 12, 22, 24-25, 36-37, 44, 45

sweatshops 5, 12-13, 15, 16, 17, 22, 24, 32, 33, 36, 44, 45

technology companies 14, 15, 16, 20, 21, 27, 41, 42, 43, 44

toxic chemicals 10, 11, 13, 28, 29, 31, 32, 38, 45

UN 4, 23, 34, 39, 41

unions 17, 23, 42

salaries 5, 12, 13, 15, 17, 19, 20, 21, 22, 23, 24, 26, 27, 37

women workers 22-23, 26

workers' rights 15, 22-23, 41

working conditions 5, 8, 9, 12, 13, 14, 15, 16, 17, 19, 23, 26, 27, 42, 44, 45